POSTER ART NIGHTS

Roy Robbins

Dedication

I would like to dedicate this book to my wife, Susan, whose support and advice, and enduring love has sustained me in every way, and our two sons, Ben and Meade, who married Amy and Cindy, who gave us Oliver, Courtney, Thomas and Remi.

And great love to Bob and Bonnie, Billy and all the Peppers, and Cathy Patton and her family.

Our dearest friends Margaret and Lou Mortimer and their children. A. S. Gilfoyle who contributed the cover photograph of the bust of Constantine, and Lindsay Nolting, whose landscape paintings provided inspiration over many years. Randi Hill at The Hill Gallery for letting poetry and painting merge.

The Virginia Center for the Creative Arts at Mount San Angelo, and Ken Jones, whose continued friendship first started there.

Live Arts Theatre in Charlottesville, and my friends at the Playwrights Lab, and Stephen Sossaman at Inkonoklast Press.

Maria Baber and all the Babers.

Amanda Meers and Jim Weber out west, and Julie and Jamie Rea down east.

Finally, Rubie Grayson at Unsolicited Press for keeping all the balls in the air.

Acknowledgements

The following poems first appeared in these quarterlies and reviews:

Northeast Journal, "Sao Paulo Evening," 1986

The Hampden-Sydney Poetry Review, "Poster Art Nights," Winter, 1996; "Why Don't   the Stars," Winter, 1998; "And Thinking to Escape," Winter, 2005

Southern Poetry Review, "The World Outside," Issue 47.1

Virginia Literary Journal, "Graduation," 2015

Awards:

"Kite Flying in a Field Near the James River," First Place, Southwest Virginia Literary   Festival

"Sunlight Variations, First Place, " Deep South Literary Festival

Table of Contents

Looking for truth but finding only

memory

DARK CITY, Charles Bernstein

POSTER ART NIGHTS

There is a ring beyond the ring around the moon.
It has the clarity of glass and contains nothing.
Not everyone can see it. But later
There will be other reproductions,
Other nights when we will watch where cars
Like beetles in the dark
Follow their twitching cones of light
Across the ridges where the river bends
Around Elk Island Farm.
But the burning spirals of my digital self
Are never just the same old song,
Each track is shorter, but contains more information,
Until the final spiral disappears untraced,
Heard only by my friend, who claims to hear
The silent 'h' in ghost.
It makes an invisible sound, he says,
Not everyone can hear it.
As on a winter night years ago we stopped here,
Angrily pulling off the road,
While the queenly moon
Assumed her listening pose across the river.
And so our words, cruel and obvious then,
Are invisible now to me,
And of the many things we said that night,
Or meant to say,
I can remember almost nothing.
Yet I still can feel
The roughness of your coat across my hands,
Still see the water drops
That streaked the steaming windows,
Drops that glittered
In the same cold light that shone
Upon the frosted blades of grass outside the car,
Both then and now.

THE STATUES

Where in the park we stood each day
By that rude philosopher with lantern thrusted high,
Who stared with his stone eyes at those who passed unheeding,
A companion girl bends now, head down, face turned away,
And gathering close her granite robes
As if his searching question had found her in a lie.
What is it that he always doesn't say
In hermetic language none of us can hear?
Like traveling without a map, you say, of dreams
That nightly took you to a silent land
Whose hieroglyphs gave meaning, instant and complete,
Which waking, you could never seem to understand.

AND THINKING TO ESCAPE

Why do we say this can't go on,
When vanishing each day at five
Through doors that open on dark streets
Impossibly we leave our spaces empty
And move cleanly westward toward the light.
Later, fumbling at the winding sheets
Sounds move past us in the night.
Though in the dark, we cannot be alone.
Something is always with us, invisible, like air
That pushes gently on an outspread sail.
It knows we must be going
And will take us anywhere,
Even to those places that 'just might have been.'
Some friends have gone before us,
We see them moving there
Like shadows in a mirror where symmetry has failed.
Awkwardly they stumble, then stare and look surprised,
As if discovered reading dead men's mail.

PROMENADE IN THE BACK YARD

The girl in brown stood by the door
      Where the bats inquired in the dusky air,
While in the yard the unwashed Poltroon
      Hacked and spit in the booted sand.

"Come out, come out, and play in the dark,"
      He plunked out a tune on his comb.
The dogs howled, and near the porch
      The cats made infrequent rushes.

But still she leaned against the door
      And made no stir. Would
That the moon had called to her,
      The moon, and the honeysuckle's drift...

GHOSTS

Only the essence in their names
Lives after them, vibrating
In the air of lonely rooms
Where once they lived.
Now, unremembered,
They are reduced to signs,
Or random noises that go unexplained.

Someone sits reading in the chair.
The summer day
Draws its strength together for the afternoon.
In the hall a floorboard creaks.
The curtains flutter
But the leaves outside are still.

In this one moment, when the reader's eyes
Lift uneasily from the page,
The mind clear but not focused anywhere,
All that is needed to bring them forth
In buzzing clarity
Is the simple murmuring of their names.

But we forget! Or quickly distracted,
We flip the page, annoyed,
And shifting in the chair
We fumble for our matches
And another cigarette.

Who will be the last to say their names?
The very last to say
"Why, this was Great Aunt Harriet's vase,
Who lived here long ago."
Then, smiling sadly,
"But of course, you don't remember her."

And what of Harriet, then?
Will she hover forever in these rooms
Like an echo,
Waiting for the one lifted sound
No traveler now on earth can make.

KITE FLYING IN A FIELD NEAR THE JAMES RIVER

I.
Two women stand at the top of the hill.
Their hands are folded
And their blue dresses are black.
Behind them a boy walks out of the sun
Descending with serious steps
His own path down the hill.
He braces a kite to the wind.
Its sharp flash startles the calves.

II.
The boy puts his kite on the ground
Then gravely steps back like a priest,
Invoking the consonant string
That goes with a hiss through the grass.
Behind him his dog like a bomb
Explodes in surprise near the cows.
Barking dumbly, she shivers for praise.
The bull flicks his drool with a chuff.

III.
Moving backward the world spins around
Like string that unloops from a reel.
The boy's eyes blur in the sun
Where astonished his feet tread the sky.
The bull's bellow has turned the hill over
So the women can stand on their heads.
Even the cows stop their chewing.
The kite's tail wags like a dog's.

ELLIPTICAL LAMENT

(For Sonny Johnson, killed by his own boat on Lake Rosa near Melrose,
Florida)

Tough Sonny went out in boat
Sporting super equipped
75 horse latest make
To show it off on Florida lake
All alone. Standing up,
Big mistake, he was flipped
Out at high speed M.P.H.
But stayed afloat,
Then, dumbly, began to swim
Toward careless boat,
Which, with motor tilted
Over, circled perfectly
Back and ran him
Down, big blades chewing
Up right leg below the knee.
Dire was it then for Sonny;
For nearby man in slow canoe
Arriving just too late at scene,
Said that for a moment after
Boat had hit him
Sonny stretched out log-like,
Floating low on lake,
Then dropped toward bottom
Spilling blood, like parachutist
In slick trick dive
Trailing long red plume of smoke,
While empty boat, uncatchable,
All afternoon like hovering drop plane
Circled over and over
Over Sonny.
Weeks later, unsuspecting

Fisherman hooked him,
Clutching rotten
At the tangled shrouds
Of sawgrass.

THE BLIND MAN

How long must I endure, old love,
The hopelessness of your returns.
Days when suddenly
Across the clouded streets you reappear,
Or there, behind me,
Reflected in a window's splintered haze
I count the passing ciphers of your face.

Though never do I turn to follow you
Like a blind man groping vaguely toward the light,
But darkly sit in empty rooms recalling
The harsh illumination of your gaze.

Leave me, then, obscure.
Too long your glittering eyes have told me
That I was not the one.

THE GREEN MAN

Deep in the snooze of summer the offspring sleeps,
Bearing his heavy, half-year dreams
That ripen toward his fall.
And winter, truly, will be the death of him,
The sodden, water-time dissolve and blend.
How, then, can spring come back again
When never did it go away,
Not anywhere. The reference was never there.
We knew it all along, but felt safe before
In saying what we liked to hear:
      "How beautiful spring is!"
                      Beautiful because
We learned its spelling early on,
And beautiful because we think somehow
That spring comes back each year.

THE LESSON

Summer is over now.
The trees have shed their weight,
And the heavy spheres of green
Resolve themselves
Into the clear distinctions of geometry.
And the forest is littered with leaves
The way the floor of Ko Sen's hut
Is littered with the discarded scraps
Of his patient, yet now unsure devising.
The light fades, and still he works,
Forgetful and alone, except where
The young apprentice kneels impatiently,
Waiting for a sign that will not come.
And after a long day
Of watching his master's failed attempts,
The boy quietly excuses himself
To find his old path once again
Through the evening air.
He observes how easily
The bare branches overhead
Form their delicate, archetypal figures
Against the enduring sky.
Why did his parents send him here!
Head bowed, hands joined behind his back,
He traces his footprints round and round,
Muttering with each step
"The art of calligraphy is dead."
Soon, he must return
And play the lackey once again
To the old man and his fumblings.

Driven by the wind, the ruined leaves
Billow and scrape across the ground,
Though all the while,
His hands more certain now,
And relieved at last of the haughty pupil,
Ko Sen copies out in haste
His final masterpiece.

THE WORLD OUTSIDE

Why don't they come
Into the room
And tell us what
We want to know?
Forte and pianissimo
Are how the rain falls, though
All at once the drops reveal
A landscape that they're falling on,
And somehow you can hear
The softness of a lawn
As you might see a picture.
Boots scrape across the floor,
But in a calm, unfretful way.
I think they're happy,
Lounging in the hall,
Standing with their coats
Half on and laughing,
Ready to come in, or step outside
And fade into the day.

WHY PEOPLE ARE SAD

1. Reflections

Habitually, we observe through difference,
Sometimes there are apples, sometimes not,
Though when we look outside
The world seems everywhere the same,

Fading away into the darkening haze
That bounds the horizon's distant edges.
It's like a puzzle that torments us!
We cannot go beyond our lives,

And though in our imagination
We skip like stones across the water
It is the actual we use to spring aloft,
But never can exceed, and even soaring

Our own reflection shadows us,
Mirrored on the surface far below,
Where we decline, helpless and enthralled,
Though dreaming always of our holiday

From the gravity of the real, as if
We could lift ourselves in some odd flight
Whose curve turned always upward
Toward a novel sphere forever free from earth.

2. What's Happening Outside

But eternity is always here, which is why
We cannot see it. If only it would vanish
And then come back again, to arrive
Like the morning train, unchanged yet obvious.

Such transformations always seem
To give us pleasure. Pigeons skitter sideways
As they vector downward, aiming for
The distant bridges on the overpass,

Flags ripple in the wind like sails
But go nowhere, while on the highways
Enameled shells of cars
Intertwine in figures that renew themselves.

And it's even more exciting in the rain,
With the deepened colors magnified
And gleaming through the clinging
Films of water; or on the sidewalk,

Where the wind pounds in a sudden backward gust
That stops the crowded pushing of umbrellas,
As, simultaneously, they all dip
In the same direction to take the blow.

3. Time For Breakfast

Out of this stylized, yet forceful air
The unexpected morning jumps at you,
Like the idiot dog, nosing under the covers
And making you spill

Your unbalanced cup of hot coffee.
Getting up, and pissed,
You turn the tap on cold
To soothe the sting.

Then to the kitchen, where you struggle
To recall if bran is au courant,
While memories of yesterday
Disassemble to that late night moment

When your mind clicked off,
Like a commercial time-out in a west coast game.
But there was no break in the action.
The circling night endured, sustaining you

In the distressing compensation of your dreams,
While the trees calmed the wind,
And the gigantic shafts of the Poles
Were turning unheard.

4. Off To Work

The Immortal Past is dead. This sounds
Unfair, though mythographers assure us that,
Quite often, familiar spirits lurk
In objects close at hand, waiting for us

Unwarily to pass by. Perhaps because of
This terrifying information, people
Go to work each day, undeterred by random gunfire,
Or the threat of widening strikes.

Though the lady on the Morning News seems baffled
As she describes the bizarre scene at the Swiss hotel,
Where, one by one, the rebel leaders jet in
To announce their new pariah state.

They are all old men, wearing wrinkled
Fifties' suits, but are surrounded by
An imposing color guard. Dressed in snappy uniforms,
They wave long knives and aimlessly parade.

Here, the economy is still declining,
Though the CEO   who fired all his workers
Has received a bonus. Happily, the death toll
From the riots is not expected to go up.

5. A Night At The Fair

Desire, for it is boundless,
Takes many forms, and we delight
Especially in those histories
Whose limits exceed the credible.

Chang and Eng, the Two-Headed Calf,
And the Amazing Gorilla Woman
Are wired in to the brain's amusement centers,
Where, compulsively, we return each night

To sail the endless reaches of the fair
As if floating on a sea of bobbing heads,
Our faces stretched in rippling mirrors
Wreathed with strings of colored lights.

And slowly we remember certain things
Beyond the cotton candy blown like clouds,
Or the marooned pitchmen with unresting eyes;
A few unlikely things perhaps,

Like the dancing waters or the elephant ears,
All blending in the discordant music
Of the midway's jangled, meditative songs,
Gay prophesies of no particular day.

6. How It All Came About

So days evaporate, and our buried lives
Emerge behind us like the ancient hills.
And looking back through the exposed strata,
We understand at last

How we evolved from our Neanderthal
Edwardian bulk, into boyish, modern suits
With stripes and pleated pants.
Preening like exotic, tropical birds,

And accompanied by spontaneous applause that grows
Into a rhythmic chant of habitual approval,
The mannequins relax into their gorgeous smiles
As they stride down the runway

Into the next millennium.
How new it all is once again!
Lights flash continually in staccato burps
Like anti-aircraft fire,

While marshaled phalanxes of flack
Transmit breathless bulletins,
As if the century were not over,
And the great wars done.

7. Refugees Are Everywhere

I will stand here watching you
At the edge of the Shouting Valley.
Figures move below like ants,
And with your binoculars you identify

Your mother, an old woman in a black dress,
Leaning on your cousin's sturdy arm.
Twice a year you fly here from the States
To wave hello, and with your homemade megaphone

Shout news and encouragement into the dry
And unforgiving desert. Others, unable
To go on, fall to their knees,
Sobbing curses into the impossibly distant nearness,

But you continue, jumping up and down
To mime encouragement, while your mother,
Like an automaton, stands beside a yellow
Warning sign, waving her arm unceasingly.

Across the hills, bringing the children
On their pilgrimage, school buses circle
The charred and broken spires
Of the burned out village where the martyrs lived.

8. The American Dream

Exiles dream of many things. Revenge,
Returns in triumph, and complete exoneration
Are often mentioned in the journals
They keep with fanatical devotion.

Immigrants, however, after many years
In the new land, remember the taste
Of their first banana. Most of us,
Living between these two extremes,

Have a drinking room where we retire
During moments of stress. I follow
My Mexican doctor's advice: two drugs
Always work better than one.

It is difficult to give up the idea
Of transcendence, the big gesture
That will redeem us forever.
Like characters in historical romances,

We pass through our heroic stages,
From shy self-abnegation to being rude
To strangers; believing all the while
That in the end, we are forgiven everything.

9. Just Another Gig

As we increase our pleasure, so we
Increase our pain, like the lead singer
In the rock group, a peroxide blond Ophelia
Who wears metallic nail polish

And makes it a point to never look
At the audience. Whining, she complains that
Even after five years she still doesn't have a label.
Backstage, we chain smoke and buy her homemade cassettes.

Going home, someone in the crowd
Wonders how she manages to sing so well
And play the cello at the same time,
Then calls her a musical freak.

Life is a bad performance. We are always
Trapped in the wrong talent pool
With the belly dancer, or the lovely singles,
Eating worms underwater, prisoners

On the mysterious islands of Reality TV.
Next month, only one returns for the finals.
How fortunate we are that death
Has such a wildly eclectic booking policy.

10. Hello Dolly

One day, as if by accident, Chance
Disappeared. At first, no one
Noticed, since the world kept changing
Like always. New shops opened,

And the boulevards contained unusual processions.
And since Chance, after all, was a woman,
We thought that she was probably sulking,
And would soon be back on the streets,

Turning, as she liked to say,
Her little tricks. She was always inventive,
And would arrange for the damndest things
To happen. Strangers would meet

At a party and fall in love, or couples,
Long married, would talk in wonder through the night
About the differences in their children.
That's when we'd laugh and say "That's Chance!"

So you can imagine how shocked we all were
When they found her body, somewhere
In Scotland I believe (of all places),
Face down in the mire of a sheepfold.

11. Those Who Believe They Are Not Deceived

I never think about language, you say,
And laugh, while the ruined muscles in your throat
Strain like syntax. Your first role
Was the clever boy with an engaging appearance,

A part you played too long, though
In Mexico City, after accidentally shooting
Your third wife with a revolver,
You triumphantly emerged as the responsible alcoholic

Who was sorry he was irresponsible, explaining
That only those who were seriously deranged
Could possibly understand. Across the chasm
Of normality, we who are not deranged salute you.

Now cancer has come, and in just a few weeks,
The Doc declares, your wasted liver
Will finally check out, sending you
Down that lonesome valley toward the sun.

You were always an ambitious child, and often quarreled
With your mother. You destroyed your voice
Out of vanity, and then became what the media allow,
A personality with a story you could sell.

12. Those Haunting Apparitions

Whenever I hear the word Myth
I reach for my gun. Just kidding!
No, but seriously, it makes you wonder
Why the idea of purity is so important.

Like the time at the party when the Baroness
Astonished everyone by giving a formal curtsy.
Except for the plastic flowers, she said,
It was a stunning evening.

After a few dances, the young,
Who dress without limits,
Moved out to the billionaire's yacht
For the real party. For them,

Only beautiful women should wear
Difficult styles and colors;
This announces that their choice is deliberate,
And not just a hideous mistake.

Never drink the wine of doubt. Embarrassed,
Your friends will quickly turn away
As you explain why your credit was revoked.
Soon, you will drift through malls, invisible.

13. Breakfast With The Big A

In the morning, after the breakfast things
Are cleared away, it seems a natural thought
To ask, "What shall I do?"
But exposed as we are to conspiracy freaks

And their consulting talk show obsessives,
What is a natural thought to us
Is to them a question of damnation,
To be examined only with the guidance

Of their inner voices. For we live,
Say these voices, in two worlds at once,
And must learn to conduct ourselves in each
According to what is required.

For though we find ourselves
At breakfast in the morning, we are
Simultaneously in the presence
Of their Lord Jehovah, who compels us

To act unthinkingly on His commands.
And our chief sin is feigning, or lack
Of sincerity, which causes night sweats,
And all the terrors of this world.

27

14. In the System

I remember reading somewhere,
Perhaps it was in Swedenborg,
That after we die nothing changes,
Our live continue like always

And the dead never realize that now
Their existence is immaterial.
This possibility has depressing side effects,
Since science now confirms

That the longer we stay in a system,
The worse we tend to perform, which gives heaven
And other post-production concepts
A pessimistic spin. We'll stay here, then,

Grinding away in the ballroom's acrid dimness,
With the speakers booming, and the giant glitter balls
Twirling in the stabbing lights.
Behind the dancers, the darkened window

Of the deejay's booth is like a mask,
Hiding whatever is going on inside.
Snapping his fingers, the promoter leans against
The wall, murmuring incessantly, "Oh Yeah!"

15. This, Just for You

I was making up a lot of this as I went along.
Probably you guessed that.
I hope I haven't offended anyone, since
So many people feel betrayed if

They can't believe that what they're reading
Didn't really happen. Let's not worry
Too much about it though,
Since I'm sure that most of you

Haven't believed this anyway.
But, now that you have reached the end,
Perhaps it's clear that many of the things
I write about are similar to those wonderful

Everyday events we encounter all the time.
It's just that poetry makes them seem more wonderful
Than they are, which is why I write it.
Others have encouraged my efforts.

Quite often, they write novels, and want me to give them
A try. But I can't write prose. I never could,
Though it took me a long time to admit it
To myself. So, there you are...

SUNLIGHT VARIATIONS

I
In the sunlight
Spider webs are floating
Across a green field.

II
Seen from a distance
The watching crows
All look one way.

III
Sunlight on the water;
Between them they create
A thing I cannot see.
IV
The one-eyed moon
Sometimes turns
Her blind side toward you.

V
Each night, bucket in hand,
The worn path through the woods
To the compost heap.

VI
One hears the wind
Differently
At night.

VII
In the moonlight
The autumn leaves
All turn one color.

VIII
Beneath the leaves
A lizard rustles
Across the path.

IX
Cattle browse in strings
Down slopes
That front the dawn.

X
Somehow, the line of hunters
Passes through
The trees unbroken.

XI
High in the trees
Cicadas sing
Of their return.

XII
In just five summers
How many will remember
The flooded corn?

XIII
Spattering across the dry field
The first drops of rain;
Black circles in the dust.

XIV
Why do green rushes
Grow out of blue water
In the old pond?

XV
Near the bank,
The log cabin where
The last slave died

XVI
After the rain
The moldering walls
Turn green in the sunlight.

THE VIEW FROM THE ARK

If only the wind had contained it,
Or if the voice had not come
Like rain through the trees,

Making the darkening clouds appear
Strangely unlucky, or if his thoughts
Had followed only the usual symmetries

And not split in the opposite way,
Then he could have sailed forever, perhaps,
Across that one amazing sea,

Across what really might have become
Only his mind, until desire
Would no longer care to make an end,

Or remember what it was like
To follow the unlonely sway of a girl
As she walked the green hills,

And not wanted to think of the answer,
As if the sky would never open,
Or the dove never return.

STONED AT THE MORNING MEETING

Faced with a need to develop the data,
The manila folders have arranged themselves
In front of plastic chairs,
And long ago, it seems, a pencil
Rolled to a stop against a china cup
Filled with the drooping bells of violets.

Sweet violets, viola adorata,
Tell me now if Audubon was happy.
Did he hum a half-forgotten tune, I wonder,
Snatched from the back of his mind,
As his brush remembered
The blue glint of life in some

Dead bird's eye?

PERSEUS

People are smart in different ways.
In the hall of stone men, a living man
Looks into his mirrored shield

As he nears the sleeping horror
At the far end of the room.
He knows that to look directly

At the truth is death, and so,
Shield high before him, he inches backwards
Along the wall, his drawn sword

Held away for silence. Nothing else moves,
Except, on the ancient stones,
At each soft step, puffs of dust

Swirl up rigid bars of light
Toward slitted windows, where, high above,
They open on the staring sun.

JUSTICE SHALLOW

1

I often try to read the Bible,
First the prophets, then the tribal,
Touching Yahweh's errant folk;
Like sheep they stray, and are often liable
Not to get the joke.

2

Romantic thought is such a strain,
It dulls the mind, yet causes pain,
And killeth wit.
Take your transcendent moment, friend,
And disremember it.

3

We should have written to Ted Hughes
About how husbands ought to choose
Between the Third's omniscient voice
And blinded First, who had no choice.

4

Someone said that all Poe's stories
Are just allegories
That take revenge on kith and kin
Just to erase his natal sin.
Mine would be so, if I were Poe.

5

Spenser, Herbert, Herrick, Donne,
Are the singers of the sun;
Shakespeare, Webster, Marlowe's devils,
Followed witches to their revels.
Milton is a special case,

The strongest voice of all his race,
The soundest ear and cleanest sense
Married to ambition's mind
And truth's intolerance.
The failure of his cause redeemed him
To humble sleep. Triumphant leave him!

6
Lowell, Berryman and Plath
Spent time in hell in the same bath,
Plath drowned, and Berryman drank,
Lowell just sank.

7
Emily and Walt are the oddest pair
Found anywhere.
All that expansion and contraction
Was not to Waldo's satisfaction.

8
Please do not forget to laugh
Before you read Swift's epitaph,
For those who suffer another's pain
Never seem to laugh again.

9
For WJC (as he leaves Washington)

There were a thousand ways for you to lie;
Then only Truth, who stands alone,
Dropped against you on the scale
Her single stone.

Chameleon Bill, whose shape conforms
To every passing scene,
Who stands on each convenient leg,
And loves what lies between;

They tell you now you must repent,
Your rod of lust be broken,
And though you never have inhaled,
You can no longer smoke 'em.

But do not fear them, artful Bill,
Nor dread Judge Starr's Talonis Lex,
They lied perverting public good,
You lied about bad sex.

10
AUDEN AT THE Y: New York, winter 1967

I heard the poet read that night
In words both various and true,
Of things that never had been said
About the things we always knew:
         How cowardice can turn our love
         Into the bitterest of gall.
He shrugged in a dispassionate way,
Then shuffled off, and that was all.

11
Self-laceration is an unassuming recreation.
The rule is, when they try it
The losers don't deny it.
The real winners
Are the silent sinners.

12
Just below the nether border
Of the world called law and order
Fearfully I flit,
Wondering how I grew distracted,
And how hope, unretroactive,
Suddenly has split.

13
War and religion met on the road,
One carried a whip, the other a goad;
I'll leave you to guess which one said
If we just work together, we'll both get ahead.

14
Sailing serenely through every depression
The rich are spreading now,
Invading even the remotest of our off-shore islands,
A plague the world can never control.
What shall we do with them, these parasites?
Those who resent the schoolchild's lunch,
And envy the widow's mite.
The answer, alas, was given long ago:
The rich will always be with you,
Persistent, like a rotting mold;
For the rich are always hungry,
The rich are always poor,
And the rich are always cold.

WILLIAM BLAKE IN THE DIGITAL UNIVERSE

As brightly all the angels shine in heaven
So do their counter-spirits burn in hell,
A universe with numbers odd and even,
Whose sequences the holy angels spell.

And their delight is endless combination,
To joy in perfect meaning that is true,
To be the one who sees the next relation,
And watch the patterns changing as they view.

But once, a number fell that had no meaning,
And, for a moment, the angels stopped their play,
Bemused to think of creatures only seeming,
Whose world is ever changing night and day.

For those confined there say that life is sorrow
And fear a darker demon they call Death,
With strict accounts against the time they borrow,
And when they speak, they struggle for their breath.

THE SHADES OF LOVERS

The twirling sprinkler forms a liquid rose
That shivers on the shadowed lawn,
Where scholars in a slow parade
Change classes down the colonnade
Where once I asked to walk with you.
And what class now do we belong to?

We are the middle citizens;
The class who knows
The non-existent class of years,
And we are those
Who sat in class where shades were drawn,
We are the class of two by two.

Though looking back it's all the same,
As if before I asked you knew
We'd play that old connecting game
Where what we walk past now is through.

THE DEATH OF PASSION

Who now
Among the dead or dying

Can ever forget
The awful and eventual end

Of that wretch,
That craven worm and king of gasbags,

Passion! His execution
Was an electrifying finale,

Edifying in its spectacle
To the ladies,

And sobering in its cruelty
To the men,

Though the children, perhaps,
Were mystified

By the strident clamor of our approval
When the sentence

Finally was carried out.
We saw them turn,

Glancing secretly at each other,
Their smiles

Strangely smug,
As if they somehow knew that

More than we could guess
Would come of this.

LIKE A FACE ON A COIN

Her Lover to the Artist

So indifferent
She seems now! Impossible,
Through muzzling darkness,
The way you uncover
Her face.

The Artist Replies

 A trick of minor abstraction,
This relic
That captures her features,
Though not the ghost of her beauty
That wantoned away with her breath.

TWO DOGS IN GEORGIA

Two dogs lie sleeping in the sun
  Circled like parentheses.
They double meaning like a pun,
  They put their noses on their knees.

Their brows are furrowed in their sleep.
  They take deep breaths and arch their backs,
Then slobber sighs that make them weep,
  And then lie still like empty sacks.

THE ISLANDS OF THE PAMPAS

(El Beni, Bolivia)

I

Swept by six month tides
The islands of the Beni revolve slowly
Under an invisible moon,
Rising in scattered archipelagoes
Above the glistening marshes
Of an inland sea.

II

I did not know
There would be dolphins in the rivers
Chattering like monkeys,
Or yellow birds rising from the island beaches
With harsh cries.

III

Bleached by the sun, the faded oxcarts
Move ponderously from island to island,
Loaded down with green bananas,
Salt, and drums of gasoline.
Their slowness can be dangerous,
Killing the drivers who are lulled to sleep.

IV

Like islands anywhere
These are inconvenient and usually avoided,
Though lovers from neighboring villages
Often use them for secret meetings.

V

The island of Juachi is renowned for orchids,
While on San Ramon
Wild pigs and parrots are often found.
Once, I met two men from Baures there.
They trotted past holding a pole between them.
Hanging by their plated tails
Were six armadillos.

VI

The Jesuits, after all,
Must have feared the islands.
Four hundred years ago
They came like Hollanders
And drained the land with dikes.
crea
Corn planted, and for a hundred years
The islands disappeared.
Then, called back to Rome,
They left the dikes to crumble.
Gradually, the water seeped back
And washed the roads away.
Soon, the islands returned.

EARLY THAW

At dawn
The pools that fill the creek
Are iced with thin
Transparent panes
That magnify the stones below.

Drop by drop
The domes of melting snow
Reveal the tangles
Of a briar thicket.

Soon the sun
And the southwest wind
And hesitant
The scraping song
Of the first cricket.

A BRIEF HISTORY OF NARRATIVE

This is a story about everything
A story is not,

And will contain
No references to a beautiful lady

Confined in a lonely tower room
That was always filled

With the fragrances of slowly ripening fruit.
Nor will you read

Of the careful way
She watched the distant sea and the town,

Waiting
For the little man who came each day

Tossing the silver balls for
Her delight.

And this is not a story about where
This country was,

Or why the King
Had imprisoned the Lady in the first place,

And the way she felt strangely compelled
Not to walk down

The unforbidden stairs and go outside,
Closing the door

Forever behind her,
With the emphasis one who writes

THE END.

WHY DON'T THE STARS

Sing hallelujah
Above the fading
Circles of light
That blur the edges
Of the room.
The fan works in the window
Pumping air
And the baby breathes
With fingers uncurled
Outside the fluttering sheets.
The summer night
Is quiet
And the last firefly
Mazily winks
Through vague trees
Unstirring
In their contentment.
And even we
Sleep noiselessly
With only our blood murmuring
We are happy
We are happy
While overhead
The praiseless stars
Burn with
No sound.

LIKE A SONG

I never thought that you would leave me,
I don't know why.
My mother said, My dear, believe me
They always say goodbye.

And now you're gone and I'm so lonely,
It's life most any way,
This emptiness because you only
Left me here one day.

SAO PAULO EVENING

The Indian woman
Who plays the blond guitar
Sits alone on the edge of the hammock
Singing, perhaps to herself alone,
Of her home beyond the Mamore,
While the other guests
Quietly talk in scattered groups
Beside the garden walls.
Then, with an unannounced hiss,
A fire balloon appears overhead
Just out of reach,
Dipping and toppling in the breeze
As it sails effortlessly
Above the upturned faces
On the lawn below.
Men leap high
Laughing as they try to bring it down,
Spilling their drinks and falling
On the flowers.
The music stops.
The woman looks up
Into the mantled light
That floats above her,
Watching the balloon
Drift in its freedom
Across the neighboring walls
And down the street.
Her raised eyes glow like altars.

A STROLL BY THE OCEAN

"It ate the food it ne'er had ate"

"How barren and uninteresting
Your face is,"
She remarked pleasantly,
"Like these beaches
Faded white
In the glare of empty noon;
Dull planes of sand and water,
With no palms."

Momentarily
He looked vaguely hurt
Like a puzzled monkey,
Then replied
"Everybody has to look
Like something."

"But how predictable!" she exclaimed,
"Like the Hamptons,
With their obvious East and West."
And in murmuring undertones
She lamented ever leaving Montauk.
"Ahh, at Montauk," she continued,
"When the land runs out,
One makes a certain choice."
Then, quickly twirling
Her umbrella like a bat,
She sent a pebble shooting
Toward some sneaking gulls,
As, splashing in the brine
With her unwarted toe,
She watched his nether mind
Run backwards like a crab.

True echo, he achieved,

Almost, her expectation,
Crying, "Yes! Let us go
To Montauk."

She smiled, as if
Somehow she could hear
The crunching sand
Inside his shoes.
"And will you drive the car?"
She questioned. "I am always
Frightened of that hill
Where the ocean
Converges on both sides
Like a coiling snake."

"Almost everybody
Is frightened of something,"
He said fearfully.

Triumphant then
She raised her arms,
Letting fall
The green silk of her scarves.
Green flowers trembled in the wind
That dyed the dazzling light,
Revealing green and distant ships
With green cascades of smoke.
"And will they be at Montauk?" she inquired,
"Those green ships at sea."

He paused, again unsure,
As once more backwards
Crablike raced his mind.
"Those ships are white,"
He said candidly,
"Like the white ships at Montauk
Waiting in the bay
With white sails."

She sighed,
And dropped her arms.
The green light faded,
And, like a dream surprised, he faded
Into astonished clarity.

And now her solitary way
Undespondently resuming,
Of clearer brow and calmer mind,
With her umbrella in her hand,
She walks along the faint
Blue line of sand
That shows the margin of the tide.

BET THE BLINDS

Beneath the arching bridge two women walking.
Shadows hiding shadows.

Six miles, now, past Bremo.
The yellow bus glides down the hill.

Mom said Uncle Jake's spiel was so good
He could sell an empty box.

To say we have a culture, then,
But to see no cultivation.

They just seem busy.
Waiting here alone, below the bottom line.

BUYING A CAR

"Hey! J.T.," I yell, "How's it going."
Hoping to surprise him as he
Waits patiently among the even rows
Of burnished cars. And J.T.'s head
Seems to swivel toward me by itself
As he squints through the glare
Thrown up by the flat white
Sidewalks that front the lot.
Then, somehow satisfied, he shifts his weight,
And coming toward me, holds out his hand
Like someone offering a dead limb.
"Good to see you," J.T. says,
And I flinch at the way he
Emphasizes good and you,
Realizing with a shock
That he is not surprised to
Find me here. I am obviously
One of those he has been waiting for,
One of those he always knew
Would turn up sooner or later.
The wind moans across the lot
And then is still, as if
A door had been unexpectedly slammed shut,
While I look stupidly around at nothing,
With my shirt sticking to my back,
And the super-heated asphalt
Baking my shoes.
Seconds pass before J.T. turns,
Gazing down the street
With his disinterested, insect eyes
To where my wrecked car
Squats like a giant, metallic toad
With its head bashed in.
"Seems like you messed up," he says evenly.

His pink, wet tongue slithers across his lips
As he winks at me like a conspirator,
And obscenely whispers
"I think there's something here you'll like,"
And before I can say no, he clamps my arm,
Walking me toward his dirty plywood shack
With its crooked "Office" sign,
While the eternal waters
Of the burning lake surge toward us
Like the incoming tide.

KISS TODAY GOODBYE

(A man of fifty, recently confined to a mental ward, can only recall his past in a fragmentary way. Watching television, and playing video games, he writes long letters to his friends, as he tries to make sense out of the disconnected images from his past, that come to his mind unbidden.)

I

I like our cafeteria sign that reads:

Ask us about
Birthday Parties
Braille Menu
Community Involvement
Educational Resource Material
Gift Certificates
Nutrition and Ingredient Information
Orange Bowl
Hospital Tours

There is a generosity of spirit here
I find contagious, and hope that soon
I will be able to ask about
Many other things. Saudi influence, the Immaculate
Conception, and the truth about the Rosenbergs
Spring immediately to mind. There can be
A liberating rapture in asking such questions,
Once you realize no answers are necessary,
A lovely phrase with almost infinite possibilities
Of interpretation, as Ethel discovered
When her brother's testimony sent her and Julie
To the electric chair. Things often
Come together in unexpected ways.
We call this an explanation, a convenient mistake
Which others, who are trained in such matters,

Encourage. For example, ask Ethel to explain
About brothers. This is the open
Unity of life many of us have come to find
So appealing; everything is related to
Everything else, or as the brilliant Reverend Hollowell
Tried to tell us that Christmas Eve long ago,
"Santa is an acronym for Satan,"
Catching us unprepared as he sent
Half the children in the congregation
Screaming out into the late December night,
As he hissed through air
Black with smoke from the kerosene stove.
He was something like a prophet, I suppose,
In the way the tabloids spoke of Orson Wells,
"He was a man ahead of his times,"
Adding the significant plural,
Which made you intensely realize
There would be more than one time
Orson would be ahead of.

                    II
I'm fighting the Numchuck Man on the third screen.
He's good, but my dropkick usually
Takes him out. Starman is next, and the last screen
Is the dreaded Pole, whom I've never beaten.
Step by step he advances with his whirling sticks,
Forcing you back toward the nightmare pit
Of scorpions. Once in, your only hope
Is to blind the bugs with laser light,
Then race them for the ladder.
I like the pills and booze. It's fun
To feel your mind go numb
And the muscles in your back let go.
But even then I'm worried, yet relaxed
In a strange way that seems
Delightful at the time, though it's getting
Harder and harder to tell where I am.
They asked the President when
He first knew about it, and he said

"I can't remember." I can't remember
Either, but people don't believe
Me. Freud's favorite joke
Was the one Mark Twain told him
Called "The First Watermelon I Ever Stole."
Twain would begin by describing how, when a boy,
He stole his first watermelon,
Then, puzzled, he would pause and say
"Why no... that wasn't the first..."
Unable to remember exactly when,
And confused by the infinite recess of guilt.
Freud would die laughing every time.
I, too, once sang and told jokes, but it upsets
Me now, the way the simulated and the authentic
Have begun to merge, like the way Mr. Palomar
Saw the grass on the infinite lawn. It was
An alien version of reality,
It was the grass without the help of point-of-view.
A child of God might see infinity,
But we can see no more
Than the flat wall of orange and purple clouds
That form behind the mountains like commercials,
Flickering across the sky before the evening news.

III
They tried to kill me in the hospital.
It was just a dream, but the letter says
I could be recalled to service at any time.
A few more data searches and my number
Will come up again. I find it very hard
To let go. It won't be easy
But I still believe that somehow
They can transfer your image to another channel.
Once there, you can read the following announcement:
        It is required that you do awake your faith.
        Then all stand still...Music! Awake her, strike!
        Now gasp and act surprised. Thank you.

Though this effect is doubtful,
Since I still suffer from the trauma
Of losing Dana Wynter to the Pod People.
Since then, my life has been guided
By the irrational desire to avoid pain.
But the critics say the films of those times
Were all socially significant,
And that a Russian invasion was intended.
Are the lights out where you are?
What if the whole building is dark
And we have to feel our way downstairs.
Nine months later, the birth rate increases
Just like Carnival. You have
A kind voice. Please look into the camera
And act sincere. Now say
"There are no Italian troops in Ethiopia."
Keep practicing until you can repeat
"My Lai is your lie," backwards twenty times.

IV

This nation was built on credit.
Many years ago businesses
Started advertising in the newspapers.
Later, they started advertising
On the radio, realizing they had discovered
A secret way to transmit my brainwaves.
Now, people all over the world
Know what I am thinking.
My only hope is to remain absolutely quiet
And think about nothing.
Spores are everywhere,
Floating in the air or growing in the closets.
I can listen to them thinking
If I remain absolutely quiet.
Or else I talk with Father Mulcahey
About the hidden messages in M*A*S*H.
So far, we agree on
The following signs, which seem to work
Much better than therapy or tarot.

Trapper is BAD NEWS, while Hot Lips
And the Colonel are JUDGEMENT CALLS,
One INNOCENT, the other GUILTY,
Depending on the weather.
Klinger, of course, is CHANGE.
If I miss the show, I remain silent
And think about nothing. It all started
With Oprah. I was watching her with friends
One day in the patients' lounge.
She and Geraldo were discussing abortion.
Suddenly she turned, and started talking
Just to me. She told me
I had to be careful, that they were on to me,
And knew what I was thinking.
Some of the voices try to trick me.
When that happens, I remain absolutely quiet
And think about nothing. I can do it
For days. Or else I sit alone,
Studying the transformations of the Holy Names
In the obituaries. I cut them out each day
And arrange them in rows on the table,
Using a system no one else can understand.
Only those who are enlightened on the seventh level
Can attain the greater meaning.
                God grant you then
                A peaceful night
                And perfect end.

PART TWO: HIS DREAM

(He falls asleep, and he dreams he is writing to a friend about a Friday
night before Christmas, long ago, when he looked down on the darkened
lights of the city from the windows of his high rise office.)

I
Someday, when we return to Christmas Town,
Grandma and Grandpa will have a warm fire
Glowing on the TV set. It will all
Make sense and be useful.
Until then, we can always enjoy
The cross-hatch pattern of the bricks
On the patio. They make a nice arrangement,
But are rumpled by ground swells
After the first frost. That is why
The rational design of this building
Pleases me. All of the arrows
Point in the right direction, and the elevators
Mostly go where they are told.
Though strange things can happen at great heights.
Once, while looking at the traffic on the bridges,
I was shocked to see some gulls
Below me, skirting among the trees and far upriver,
In search of untapped garbage I suppose.
Sometimes, too, there are false alarms
When vague messages are bruited on the intercom.
Then we are told that "The upper levels
Need not evacuate the building at this time."
Only at such moments am I afraid,
Though they reassure us that in a real emergency
We would be the first to know.
Bubble are made of air, but for us
These fragments of our lives are real
And need to be examined carefully
In case a moral might be found. For example:
      Some carpools last for twenty years
      With the same occupants.

And still the setting sun
Flames its orange streamers westward
In the cold December sky.

II
Yet the eye is directed by emptiness
To the forms of the city, just as in physics
One can speak of light and heavy holes.
These are minus devices, where Nothing
Serves as a sign, and can be measured,
Of course, in negative numbers.
Everybody has to take direction, to move off
Toward home at the end of the day.
You always feel better after the milk and oreos.
"I see you are still alive!" someone shouted
From a passing car to a friend
Standing on the sidewalk. Oh joyful
Recognition! And she, relieved to feel
Self's wave of sudden pleasure
Waved back in such a cheery style
That I could almost hear the sleigh bells
Jingle, I am alive...live...live...
Do spirits move among us? People
Keep asking about ghosts.
Are there negative forms as well as
Negative numbers? What lights up the world
Is not the Self, but the rhythmic
Repetition of the names. Names
Calling to other names, and other
Names calling to others still beyond
In an endless chain that allows you to move
Off in another direction toward
Anything at all.

III
Wink out, great eyeball. It is time
To feel the Christmas spirit move among us.

It is time to go home.
What's wrong with kind old Santa, anyway?
He is not here but far away.
Santa has decided to move off
In another direction. Santa
Is not a ghost. Only disconnect your sleigh,
Old man, and tell us your problems.
And querulously Santa complains, "D'ere ist
Too many names of tcheldrun in de vurld."
The mainframe is my model here.
A system dump prints out the universe
But baffles the mind with abundance.
Do you remember that scene in the "Cherry Orchard?"
Somewhere a string breaks suddenly with a twang
That is heard by everyone at the picnic,
(Be not afear'd. It is not you, old heart.)
And in another scene we find out a cable broke,
Sending the bucket crashing to the bottom of the mine.
Events make sense, but not all events
Can be slipped on the same string of beads
Or the string will break. That is why
This building pleases me, and that is why
I'm going home. It is my desire
That moves me. My desire is not
My self. Myself that moves
Alone now to the windows high above
The city, where the Great Day is exhaling
In a sigh of fumes.

IV
Imagine, then, that you are here alone with me
In this building on Friday night.
Christmas is approaching and you are tired.
The day was long, the week was even longer,
And the year interminable. Old friends are gone.
Below, the traffic copter thumps by one last time
Over the stalled cars on the freeway.
Across the ceiling in black waves

Long banks of lights go down, and somewhere,
Behind partitioned walls, janitors begin their rounds
Of ordinary exorcism.
There is nothing more to say, and yet somehow,
You sense there is a spirit here,
Unnamed, disconsolate, and pitiable. It is not
Santa Claus. Rather, it reminds you of the beep
Your new digital watch makes
Every hour, a sound regular and plain
Like this building. Listen for a moment,
And try if you can hear, above
The distant hum of vacuum cleaners,
The year's Epiphany begin magnificat.

V
Night blackens the windows, and one by one
Levels are secured and then abandoned,
Leaving only dim, red bulbs
Glowing beside the stairwell exits.
Silently, the phones nod their heads,
And pencils, enclosed in their delicate, yellow skins,
Sleep chastely on brown envelopes
Arrayed in overlapping rows like venetian blinds.
All the desks in the building are quiet.
Mutely attentive, charts and maps
Lie open on the tripod legs of metallic stands,
As if waiting for some final strange command
To prophesy in varied tongues. What angels,
Gleaming and forever young, will finally appear
Among these shards
Of gummed notes and half-erased names,
And swaying gently to the electronic incandescence
Of the neon strobes, dance in waving files
Around the burning heaps of inter-office mail.
Transcendent, their bare feet
Will pound the carpet's garish, artificial green
And lift the razored particles of silicon
Into a whirling toxic cloud above their heads.

Ecstatic, they will chant of work and freedom,
And their music have such power
That Reason, summoned in her chariot of fire,
Will ride across this maze of paneled walls
With bolts of lightning, shattering forever
The obscene rows of modular furniture
Into unique flakes of beneficent
Plastic snow.

PART THREE: WHAT HE COULD REMEMBER

(He wakes, and as the hospital day resumes, he begins another letter,
moving in his mind toward the one clear memory he has been able to
retain, Kennedy's inaugural, where he rode on a float at the end of the
parade.)

I
"El Salvador is Spanish for Viet Nam."
I write this to all my friends, insulting
No one. People ask me, "How do you
Know these things?" And I answer
That I don't know. "But how do you
Know that you don't?" they continue.
I want to say that there is no answer.
All of us have to take our chances.
With bored expressions, I watch them turn away,
Looking out the window for a hero.
I'd give a lot to own a tuxedo
And go to fancy places,
Like a black swan among the pigeons.
I can tell you understand,
But want me to explain it anyway.
The truth is that I am much like you,
And look for heroes everywhere.
But it's all so pleasant now. The birds
Are singing, and the organist has begun to play
The Wedding March. "Can we have the ring?"
Someone asks. There is applause,
And then the distant sound of gunshots.
The grass turns red.
Terrorists are everywhere, and perhaps
This is not the time to be exposed.
Inside the box there are always surprises,
And we can see now why it was necessary
To blow up the hotel. For the faithful,
He was an honest-to-goodness king

And atonement was required. Only then
Could he return to claim the throne.
The problem, as I recall,
Has to do with ventilation. It's the smell
That bothers us at night. Perhaps
The hospital furnace isn't working properly,
Or what if this really is a dream?
When I wake up, my analyst has promised
To give the bride away. Shall the dead be razed?
Let us kneel together here upon the grass
And say our prayers.

II
There was another top-level change
In the Cabinet today. When the riots
Began, the government security forces
Arrived in trucks and opened fire.
All of the rebels were killed, except a few,
Who unaccountably escaped, and are hiding
In the countryside. Dressed in new fatigues,
Fidel stepped out of the car and went inside.
He has just learned that the latest data
Show that the poor don't like to be hungry.
They have captured the mystical City of Light
And are eating their way toward the Capitol.
Where are they now, the "Beautiful People"
Larger than life who filled our dreams?
Have you found the key? Someone said
It has the same shape as Johnson's scar.
Yet how comforting they are,
Those royal blue and white signs
That mark the Eisenhower inter-state highway system.
Shhh! Be quiet. Did you hear a noise.
What is out there, Lyndon, hiding
Beneath the foliage, and waiting
For our troops to come a few steps closer.
Jump in the chopper and get us out of here.
All roads lead away from the hungry people

Toward something shining before us in the night
With Grecian clarity. Something familiar,
Like the white marble of the Parthenon,
Guiding us in the darkness like a beacon
Where Pennsylvania dog-legs right and left
Past bronze Mr. Hamilton and Jackson's deft salute.
It is all coming back, and I remember
Everything at last. And we are ready now
For our brief moment to occur.
Kennedy's children changed the world,
Didn't they?

III
Let the coda begin! It is time
To pour out the Bardic syrup
Across the page. Other people do it,
So why should I feel ashamed.
Not everybody can be good all the time.
By popular demand I know longer play
The clarinet. Plato, however, did not
Cut and paste, and I can promise that,
In the end, everything will be explained.
   DRUM ROLL   DRUM ROLL   DRUM ROLL
Is this beginning to sound more regular?
Can you hear the verses galloping
Down the stretch toward the Resolution
At the finish line? Are you ready for me
To make an announcement? Are you ready for me
To jump off the page and grab you by the throat?
Wouldn't it be thrilling if I did.
And isn't that what secretly you most desire?
Everything I know about you tells me
I am right. And everything
You know about me reassures you.
You know that I am dying to do it,
Dying to give it to you hard and fast,
Until the tears come, and you cry aloud
With...pleasure? So, here it is:

           "And then my heart with pleasure fills
           And dances with the daffodils."
Brush the tears away, luv. I'll turn
My back until you're finished. We all
Need our little fix to get us through the day.
I myself prefer the last few pages
Of detective stories. But, as my nephew says,
Whatever floats your boat.

PART IV

JANUARY, 1961: THE INAUGURAL PARADE

It snowed the day before the Inauguration,
And morning saw a dawn
Of intense cold, with a sky
Purged of history to a pale, clear blue.
Everything was new. We were starting over.
Dressed like mountain men,
My friend and I were Lewis and Clark
Standing in frozen awe before Sacajawea
(Portrayed by one of the real Indians)
Who pointed toward the end of the float
At the imaginary mountains. Behind us,
Wearing moccasins and breach clouts,
A small band of Apaches unbraided
In a continuous, shuffling dance.
All day we waited at Columbus Circle
While the parade, led by a raucous band
Of Boston fireman, gradually uncoiled itself
Down Pennsylvania Avenue.
We cheered them wildly as they stepped out
On the long march toward the reviewing stand.
"In an hour it will be our turn!"
My friend yelled over the booming drums.
But the Boston boys marched down and back
Before we moved an inch.
And still we waited through the bitter afternoon,
Legs spread and freezing slowly into poses
Like abandoned sailor ice-bound at the Pole.
Then, just at dusk, and beyond despair,
Across the Circle like a thrilling drumbeat
Our orders came:
    YOU...MUST...PREPARE
    YOU...ARE NOT...FORGOTTEN
    HE...IS WAITING FOR YOU...NOW
Unbelieving, but revived by gulps of whiskey,

Our drivers fired their engines,
And lunging like drunk elephants
We drove through crowds now leaving in the dark,
And flowing backward in black waves
Up Capitol Hill. Near Grant's brooding statue
We stopped, while a high school band,
So cold they couldn't play a note,
Fled groaning like a defeated army, pursued
By the unrelenting wails of majorettes.
More jerking stops and starts, until
With a deliberate motion of his arm
A trooper waved us forward,
And majestically out we rolled,
Following the lines of bobbing lights
That disappeared into the whitened darkness.
We were the very, very last of all that great procession.
Behind us, our Apaches threw off their robes,
And with a shout began to dance,
Jumping miraculously through turquoise hoops
While poised above a swaying platform
Of bronze and silver foil. In the dark and cold
We moved past empty stands
Where TV cameras drooped unattended,
Our only audience a few mounted policemen,
Breath steaming and impatient to go home.
Braced against the wind, I prayed,
While Sacajawea pointed toward her mountains.
Please God, I moaned, let him still be there.
I don't give a damn if it is cold,
Just keep him warm a few more minutes
And I'll never bother you again,
But please God, just so I can say
He saw us when we passed. He gave a sign.
Past Hancock's statue and Fourteenth Street,
Past the Hot Shoppes and the old Willard Hotel,
My feet shifting in agony
As we turned at Treasury, and nearer now,
A swell of noise, and suddenly, encased in light,
The magic bubble of the reviewing stand,

Glass sparkling against a jet-black sky.
The iron spears on the White House fence flashed by
And we were there, slowing down
Where he stood waiting, outside in the cold, alone.
He was dressed in formal black, and we passed
So close that I could hear him say distinctly,
"Very good." He doffed his hat
Just as we drew even. Had I reach out
I could almost have touched him
With my hand.

FOR S...

Complete at last our lyric love,
These sentimental fictions seemingly unfeigned,
Contradict themselves with detailed fuss.
But the world goes on without us.
It cannot be contained,
These ardent measures no song can prove.
Where are we if our sentenced days
Are infinite in their address.
The calculus of the sliding sun
Moves through our hearts like stone.
Only together can our numbers raise
A harmony of airs in unison.
Terminus we sing alone.
The greater measure is what we have done.

THE OLD WOMAN AND ACHILLES

The old woman in the bedroom reading Greek
  Fumbles the pages of her Homer slowly.
The once spoiled cat sleeps near her chair
  Like Briseis forgotten after all that wrangle.

She thinks how great Achilles was tripped down,
  Then smiles, remembering a time and place
When it was she who lightly danced,
  As if all gravity were changed to grace.

GREETING CARDS

Relationships are hard to understand.
But if we need some help
The racks of cards are always in the drugstore,
Like the matrices anthropologists devise
To diagram kinship permutations.
Ordering the columns across the top
Are names for all the great occasions;
Birthdays, Death, Christmas, the lover's Valentine,
While brother and cousin, wife and niece,
In cross-reference down the side,
Stand ready to assume the various masks
Appropriate to the season.
The colors are usually bright and cheerful,
Though they often come in the slightly drabber shades
Our aunts call tasteful, forcing us
To buy them when they send us out to shop.
But life is like that.
And next week at the party, there will be flowers,
And a figure who sits in the center of the room,
Someone who is happy to feel important,
But acting embarrassed as she says that, finally,
We have given her too much.
Then, opening our large, square envelope, she removes
The robin's egg blue card with the lace borders
And reads the inscription aloud,
Before she looks around to fatefully exclaim,
"Now isn't that sweet!"

HUCK AND POLITICAL CORRECTNESS

(Fragment of a letter from Huck to Judge Thatcher)

...and so I told
Our social pragmatics teacher, Mrs. Brigham,

I wasn't trying
To be insulting when I said

The world could kiss my multi-cultural ass.
But Mrs. Brigham said,

Yes, Huckleberry, on one level this phrase
Is insulting, coming,

As it does, out of an offensively vulgar
Form of popular

Discourse, in which you are clearly proficient,
Since you often use it

To generate strings of similar common expressions,
Slicked over with

A crudely devious
Sense of humor designed to hide

Just where
The power of the classroom really is.

And I said
I wasn't trying to hide anything,

But before
I could say something else,

Mrs. Brigham raised
Her hand, and with a kind of sickly smile

Pointed out how it was painfully obvious
To everybody

That I couldn't hide a glass of water
In the Mississippi River,

And how in the future, I ought to stop
Interrupting her, since

Any fool could see
How a simple first level phrase like mine

Had to presuppose
A higher level of meaning like hers

That was better,
And this was why smart people

Could always make things come out right
In the end.

Now, Tom's Aunt Polly is saying
That I have to

LEAVE SCHOOL AND GO TO WORK!

And I was just
Wondering if you might have

Some kind of handy job for me to do
Down at the Courthouse

FOR MY DARK LORD

Were I to see my own death date, and know
The now uncertain limits of my life,
Would this foreknowledge bring death to my soul
Before my bodies death? And would I grow
Into some casual creature, freed from the strife
That hope engenders, living free of any goal?
For surely my dark lord will claim as fee
This piece of earth that I but hold today,
And keep as fief upon his constancy,
A tenant whom he soon will send away.
What matter, then, for me to know the hour,
When soon or late I know that he will come,
As I do see, prefigured in a flower
That roses all will fade, and mouths grow dumb.

A LIFE IN SNAPSHOTS

Flipping through the pages of her album
One is quickly seduced by the glamour,
The sense of voyeurism,
And the palpable warmth of the famous people
Who danced in and out of her life
During the last seventy years.
Many, of course, have disappeared.

From the beginning, she was sure
That she would never marry,
And was funny and self-deprecating
About her weight and off-center nose
Like a female sidekick in the TV sitcoms.
Then, in a sudden career move spin-off,
She discovered the camera, and quickly realized
Her talent for making people
More interesting within a frame.

And she was free, then, to become
Indifferent to beauty. She could drink
All that she wanted, and take more photographs
That never lied about people.

CONSERVATION

Within your hand you hold my book.
Open it and take a look.
What you find will not be you,
You lay beyond what I could view,
Nor will you find, alone yet free,
The one my analyst and I called Me,
Just who Me was they never said,
Though all the while both took my bread,
And told Me how life's really tough,
And that I never felt guilt quite enough.
For happily the fates construe
That all we dream is what we knew,
But had forgot or just misplaced.
In truth, we are a thoughtless race,
Surprised to learn that all we know
Are picture stories from a show,
Where choices that we seem to make
Are sequenced so there's no mistake.
A scene where depressive Mom and Dad
Are the best pals you never had,
And kindly, curious Uncle Fred
Would wait until you went to bed,
Then pinch your arm until it bled.
And they're still there, the whole damn crew
With lists of things for you to do,
Insisting that you can't forget
Those things that haven't happened yet.
It's like first grade, you'll be just fine
If you can learn to stand in line.
The Fuhrer got it right; to marchers
He thundered, "There are no departures.
Just follow orders like your fathers."
The future? No one really bothers.

NIGHT RADIO

How into unexpected music once you broke.
I remember.

And there were other times recovered,
Like the scent

Of flower petals, left decaying in a jar.
Vacancy would take me then

To a stretch of lonely road at night,
Where my thoughts

Click off and on: Who am I? For a long,
Long time

Only the silence speaks. All over now,
And emptied out

By love, I listen
As your voice grows dim, then fades away.

You played
Your silence with the surest touch;

I had the last word, and usually
Proved right,

But dearly paid for hearing far
Too much.

GREEN FIGURES

At the beginning of beyond
The real is waiting,
Like the froth left floating on the pond
After the wind and snow.
All over now, no place to go,
We stumble on,
Except for you
Who lingers, searching for a sign,
And lifts a shout
Where the green tips
Of the first daffodils appear.
What is so surprising here
Is how safely we can move again
Finding ourselves enclosed once more
Within another year,
Although, we soon recall,
That at last summer's end
It was great death who came
And cut away each thing
Whose time it was to fall.
Should we not tremble so?
His power is beyond us all.
We count by day and night
The changing dark and light,
A calculus for things that never stay;
Let these recurrent numbers, then,
Invoke our tuning rhyme,
Somehow,
Metonymy is endless time
And metaphor is now.

RECURSIVE

Everything can be explained
Except the explanation,
Otherwise, who could understand anything?
Does it really
All come back to haunt you,
Or is there a way
Out that allows you to
Finally get out
Of the way in time,
And avoid the expected backsliding surge
Of guilt, where you always feel that,
At last, you really understand,
Even as someone is telling you how
 The evidence
Has your fingerprints
All over it,
Which helps you realize
That, now, you probably are ready
To accept the situation.
Afterwards, you will feel
Much better.

GRADUATION

(At a small college in the American South)

So the bright day called to us, and cried aloud,
Saying, Look! Look at this light, and witness
Through these shimmering, transparent panes
And be glad. And so we did, and so we were,
And holding hands in our community,
We strolled across the bright grass
To where we filled our plates with Cole slaw,
Rolls, and barbeque, before sitting down
With the converted multitudes,
By the edge of the artificial lake.
The beautiful women then assumed
Their positions of adornment to the scene,
While the men lounged and listened,
And all of the mothers stood up
When they were told to stand up,
And a little girl sang in clear tones
About how this was the time to let go. Then,
The greater oracles who had been summoned appeared,
And prophesied that only those
Who listened to their inner voices
Could possibly achieve their desires,
And in murmuring affirmations
We all agreed that this was good.
But then the sky darkened, and an unstoppable wind
Blew the plastic plates and cups across the lawn,
As a voice of unexpected anger filled the sky,
Shouting, "The great god Pan still lives!"
And terrified, we arose, to scatter in all directions
Like the silly flocks of the field.

ANOTHER FAILED HOMAGE

I was going to tell you something special
About the world we live in,
Something about the way my garden has
Of miraculously renewing itself each year,
And how writing poetry is like tending a garden,
And I wanted to explain why it seemed so important
For me to be the one to tell you about my thoughts,
Since that is what poets do when they have feelings
That are often called transcendent.
But then I started watching the fan on my ceiling,
With its blades slowly turning in a continual blur,
And I grew dizzy and almost drunk, you might say,
And something in my mind reached out,
And then was gone, and I became almost nothing
Except someone watching the blades of the fan
Slowly turning on the ceiling above my head.

I SAW YOU SPINNING LIKE A TOP

I had gone out into the night
To retrieve your coat

And forgetting where we parked
I searched the lot

And hummed a tune
That echoed from the ballroom

Where I had left you sitting
At our table with some friends.

Then, growing more and more discouraged,
I found myself, without realizing it,

Next to a window, and watching the dancers inside
As they turned to the music.

And for a moment, I circled within their circles,
Becoming one with them,

Until I saw you dancing there,
Not sitting at our table as I supposed,

But with a stranger's arm about your waist,
And spinning in one place,

With the folds of your lavender dress
Whirling around your knees,

And your face transfigured by the ecstasy you found
Within the music.

And I felt the desolation as it entered my heart,
For I could see l how your life might be

Were I to die, and how you would go on without me
As if I had never been.

I fell back, then, as from a sudden blow, and blinded
I stumbled away

Toward a darkened place beneath some trees
Where I could not be seen.

Eros, who brings together and divides one soul
From the other,

Do not show me this again.

HEADING WEST

The rain began last night
We both agree it won't be missed

Carrying our bags, we walk to the car
Wearing our recently faded jeans

Did we forget the dog's new medicine
We do not go back

The wet tires hiss
As if resisting our departure

They say that on the high plateau
The wind turns brown

Colorado can't be that different
Let's buy a travel magazine

What do they talk about out there
Brush fires and skiing don't seem to go together

What about, Let's have a toke,
I suggest. A pause.

You laugh and say, It sounds exciting,
Once you get used to it

Calls of travelers mingle in the air
With tense, inertial shrieks of trains

Standing on the marbled floor
You look for pictures in the grains

You see a snake, a blob with rabbit ears
And finally a woman in a veil

I laugh and say, Which one shows our future
Afraid to guess, you turn away

THE LAND OF MY LAST DESIRE

Living, as I do, under the sun of my own existence,
I like to slide the intensity bar all the way over to the right,
Which makes all the objects on the screen fade out
Into a bright, invisible light that hides everything.
Imagining this counter-intuitive world pleases me,
Since I normally think of our visible, everyday reality
As vanishing into an enveloping darkness that leads
To my unconscious mind on the other side of sleep.
Or something like that. At any rate, it is the brightness
That lures me on, always increasing my desire to visit once again
This indistinct land of a light so painful, that I can enter only
By walking backwards, shielding myself from looking into
An omni-present burning eyeball as I move slowly across a terrain
Littered with the detritus of a life that I have yet to live,
Where I can identify things only after I move past them,
And, by then, they are irretrievable. And yet, somehow
I like it here, inching always backwards as I watch
The events of my life clarify themselves behind me
Until they recede into the light that never fades.

DEGAS' WOMAN IN THE ROUND TUB

Lady in the round
Bath bending down
With swing of hip
And bundled hair
Your freedom is my leisured stare
That holds you here
Until you stand and turn
And swing again lady
In the round
Bath bending down.

WHAT WE CAN'T CONTROL

I dreamed last night you went away
To be with your old love once again,
The cruel man who calls to you
Across the chambers of my mind.
And why you go to him I cannot say,
I only know it causes endless pain,
And though I plead, you never stay,
My strength is straw,
And all my thoughts are blind.
So every night I sorrow at your going,
Aware of all that always is past knowing.

www.ingramcontent.com/pod-product-compliance
Lightning Source LLC
Chambersburg PA
CBHW031143090426
42738CB00008B/1204